Sincerely, YOU

LETTER-WRITING to CHANGE the WORLD

Savannah Maddison

Rodale Kids 🌱 New York

Text copyright © 2019 by Savannah Maddison
Cover art and interior illustrations copyright © 2019 by Jill De Haan
Additional interior illustrations by Michelle Cunningham

Rodale and the colophon are registered trademarks and Rodale Kids
is a trademark of Penguin Random House LLC.

Visit us on the Web! rhcbooks.com

Educators and librarians, for a variety of teaching tools,
visit us at RHTeachersLibrarians.com

Library of Congress Control Number: 2018018610

ISBN 978-1-63565-355-7 (trade) | ISBN 978-1-9848-9371-0 (lib. bdg.) |
ISBN 978-1-63565-356-4 (ebook)

MANUFACTURED IN CHINA
10 9 8 7 6 5 4 3 2 1
First Edition

Contents

INTRODUCTION

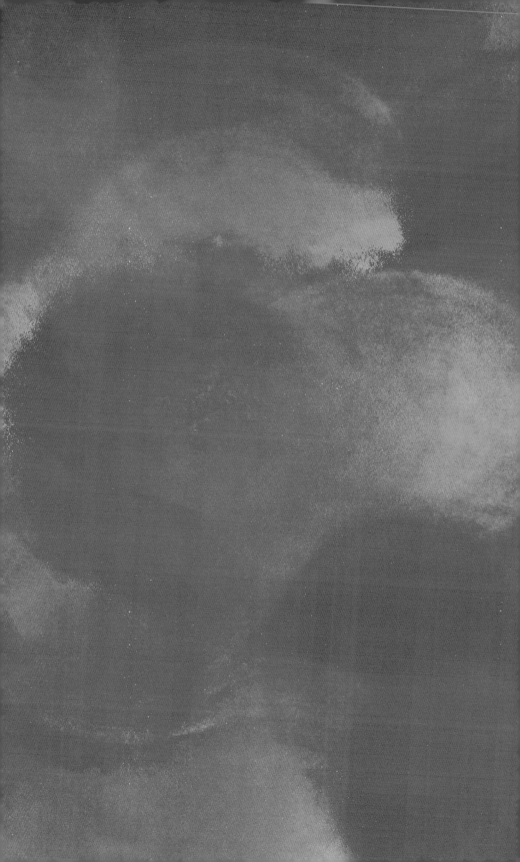

Bridges have a lot of meaning to me. Big bridges, small bridges, wood bridges, metal bridges, old bridges, and new ones—I love them all. Every time I see a bridge, I think about how that bridge is an important link. It connects two places, the "here" to the "there."

Life is filled with small, meaningful connections, just like bridges. A photograph, a video, a piece of art, or a handwritten letter connects people through shared memories, feelings, desires, and dreams. In many ways, these small connections represent some of the strongest and most fundamental pillars of our society. They stand for love, for community, for teamwork, and for the freedom to be who we are, believe what we want, and do the things that make us happy.

For kids living in the United States, freedom is one of those bridges that connect us all. Every day, many men and women leave their families behind to protect our freedom. They sacrifice so much for us. Just think about all the time they are away from the people they love. Think about all the important moments they miss out on because they are away from home. They are true heroes.

But as much as we need them, they also need us.

My journey began with a pen and a piece of paper. In the fifth grade, my best friend, Wilson, told me her father was being deployed, a word I didn't quite understand at the time. Once I learned what it meant, we wrote him a letter to show him how much we cared.

Because of that first letter, and with the help of thousands of kids like you, I started a charitable organization called Savannah's Soldiers. At Savannah's Soldiers, we engage kids in our national letter-writing campaign to send "Dear Hero" letters to deployed troops around the world. Our mission is to help kids create change in the world around them, with a special focus on supporting our military and veterans with pride. Our programs and performances raise awareness about how much the military and their families do for us every day, in ways we can't always see.

COUNTLESS KIDS HAVE CHIPPED IN, AND TOGETHER WE HAVE WRITTEN OVER 250,000 LETTERS ADDRESSED TO SERVICE MEMBERS WHO DESERVE OUR APPRECIATION AND GRATITUDE.

Many of these men and women are far away from their loved ones, and the letters are reminders that we are thinking about them. Our goal is to send one million letters, so I hope this book inspires you to send your own letter. We need your help!

I never thought something as easy as writing a letter could make such a huge difference in someone else's life, but I have seen the amazing results firsthand. Writing letters, just like crossing bridges, connects people and fosters a really strong bond.

When someone you love goes away even for just a little while, it can feel like a part of you goes with them. Almost like you've lost a part of yourself. It's hard to stay on your path when you feel like you're alone. It's not an easy spot for anyone to be in. And a letter written to your faraway relative or friend is just the start. More than anything, writing a letter builds a bridge from "here" to "there." Once you cross that bridge, you can look back at where you came from to realize you were never alone.

But sometimes it's not easy to figure out what to say. Sometimes it's hard to feel like you're still close when someone is so far away. Quick texts and emails don't capture everything you're feeling—lonely, proud, sad, scared. Nothing is worse than trying to tell someone something that really means a lot to you and knowing that you're failing to get your true feelings across. How do you write about missing your dad when you can't find the words? How do you explain to him that you can't make mac and cheese as yummy as he does, even though Mom swears you're doing it right?

I'm here to help you realize that maybe it's not as hard as you think to get these feelings down on paper—there are truly a number of ways to express how you feel, *especially* when you're feeling so sad, or missing so hard, or feeling so conflicted. There's no wrong way to do it, and I'm going to get you started. You might be surprised by what you learn about yourself and your passion along the way—just like I did.

· · · · · · · · · · · · · · · · · · · ·

Men build too many walls and not enough bridges.

— Joseph Fort Newton

· · · · · · · · · · · · · · · · · · · ·

Writing a letter used to be the only avenue to connect with people who weren't near you. It is a lost art of sorts. But a handwritten letter is a beautiful and unique expression of your feelings. You can be creative, funny, colorful, or silly, and really let your personality shine through. You can keep letters and read them again and again. Giving yourself that space of a page (or a few pages) lets your creativity soar. And let's face it: Finding a handwritten envelope addressed to you shoved between all those catalogs and bills in your mailbox just brightens your day.

This book is for anyone who is lonely or scared, or who is missing a best friend, a parent, a grandparent, or another loved one. It's for quiet nights, confusing days, or any time you want to express something complicated to yourself or the world around you. It's for the kids trying to make their dreams a reality and live up to their purpose in life. It's for our troops who are serving our country every single day. It's for you and me.

So grab your pen, your paper, and even some red, white, and blue markers. I hope this book helps you feel ready to find new ways to connect to the world around you, build friendships and relationships with the people you love, and really make a difference in the lives of those who need it the most—one letter at a time.

xoxo,

CHAPTER I

Finding Inspiration

The First Letter

It all started with my best friend, Wilson.

I met Wilson in the fourth grade. She had blond hair and blue eyes—just like me. We liked all the same things, and we would sit by each other at lunch. We became really close, really fast. Wilson and I were always talking, laughing, and sharing secrets with each other. You just couldn't keep us quiet when we were together.

One day at school, Wilson walked up to me on the playground and I noticed she seemed really sad. She looked at me and said, "I think my dad is being deployed to Afghanistan, and we're going to end up moving to Georgia." I had no idea how to respond.

I couldn't believe it. I knew Wilson was very close with her dad, and we were inseparable.

I didn't even know what the word "deployment" meant. That day after school, I sat down with my mom and searched for the definition online. For an hour, I watched videos, read articles, and thought about my best friend. That's where I learned the true meaning of the word.

It meant her dad would be sent to a place he had

never been and would probably never go otherwise, and he might not even be able to tell her exactly where he was. He might be risking his life, and he might be saving lives. He might be too cold; he might be too hot. We were in fifth grade at the time, and she knew she probably wouldn't see him again until middle school, which seemed so far away. Wilson didn't know what her dad would be doing each day, or if he could call her or text her. He wouldn't always have access to a computer to send emails, since he might be in the desert or living in a small town without a lot of technology.

I had always known there were soldiers fighting in many different ways for the USA all around the world, but it wasn't until I talked to Wilson that I learned exactly what that meant for the rest of us. I knew how much I'd miss Wilson, and I was starting to realize that Wilson felt the same way about her dad. I wanted to help.

That's the MOMENT REAL

BUILD a

HERE T

I
...IZED ... that
I HAD TO
BRIDGE from
THERE.

I've always loved music, and my dream has always been to be a performer. I wanted to cheer up Wilson in the best way I knew how, so I decided to write her a song. I'll tell you more about that later, but I'll just say that even though the song was awesome and we listened to it together all the time, I felt like something was missing. Wilson was still sad, and I knew the song wasn't enough.

I sat down and talked to Wilson's mom. I needed help figuring out what to do. She told me that even though we couldn't text or call Wilson's dad, we could send reminders in the mail: care packages, letters, anything we could create and stuff inside an envelope or a box. Then an idea hit me: If I could write a song for Wilson, why couldn't we write something for Wilson's dad? I knew that letter-writing was a great way to stay connected to someone long-distance, but I had never tried it before. Wilson loved the idea!

Then I thought, "What if we find out how many soldiers will be there with Wilson's dad, and we write them all letters? Me and Wilson, and other kids from our class and neighborhood." I figured most of these soldiers would really like a handwritten letter once they saw that Wilson's dad got one. We didn't want them to feel left out, and we thought it would be cool for them to talk with each other about the letters they received and even who had sent them. It would help build camaraderie, make them smile, and distract them in their downtime.

I got to work on the letters. I asked my close friends and kids from around my neighborhood to help me. We'd all meet after school at my kitchen table and write and color until we had thirty letters in a pile, ready to go. We were so excited to send the letters. But then we found out that Wilson's dad's unit had over seven hundred soldiers! We were so far away from our goal. Seven hundred letters a month was going to be a major challenge.

I couldn't just give up, so I decided to get help from other kids in my school. First, I asked the class next to mine to write letters. When that was successful, I moved on to the next class! Eventually my whole school was writing. When that wasn't enough, I went out to get help from other schools in our area. I started going to churches and youth groups and asking for letters. The teachers helped to spread the word, and it became a really cool South Florida initiative, eventually spreading throughout the rest of Florida, Georgia, and Alabama.

I couldn't believe it. With each letter, we connected one of these faraway men and women to their homeland.

I learned a lot about the military during this time. I learned that the military isn't just a group of people with guns and grenades. They are moms, dads, sisters, brothers, grandparents, and friends. I also learned that service isn't just about being at war. Soldiers are highly trained mechanics, doctors, nurses, engineers, scientists, drivers, and so much more. They help communities by building roads and schools. They dig wells and deliver supplies, such as food and water, to those in need. They are specially trained and ready at a moment's notice to do whatever our country asks of them. When they join up, their entire family serves, not just the soldier. Their sacrifices are also their amazing triumphs.

I hoped to show these brave men and women as much support as I could. They help us so much, and all I wanted was to help them back. I realized that writing letters lets us reach across the miles and stay connected by finding ways to share the moments that make every day meaningful—the first leaf of autumn, a lyric of a song, a guitar string made into a brace-let, a silly picture, a secret wish, or a private fear. I hoped that by receiving letters, the soldiers would be reminded of why they'd left to fight for our country in the first place. Each letter would build a meaning-ful bridge from here, reaching all the way to there.

Writing Your First Letter

So how do you get started? There are tons of ways to do this, but I find it's good to start with the absolute basics. If you are ever stuck and don't know what to write, you can always come back to these tips.

THE SALUTATION

The first part of any letter is a salutation. "Salutation" is a fancy way of saying "greeting." All the letters that come through Savannah's Soldiers are addressed "Dear Hero," because everyone serving in our military is a hero! The most classic start to a letter is "Dear." It's a beautiful word that shows you care. What if you want to be playful? What if you want to be formal? Here are some words to choose from to get you started:

Hello!

Hi, I hope you are doing great!

Dear Hero

(if you're writing to a military member)

What's up?

Greetings from snowy Nashville!
(that's where I live)

Bonjour!

To Whom It May Concern

¡Hola, amigo!

If you're still stuck, close your eyes and imagine seeing that person after a long while apart. What's the first thing that you want them to know?

THE BODY

Next, you get to start writing the body of the letter. "Body" just means all the stuff between the beginning and the end. I like to aim for three paragraphs in the body of my letter. But you can do whatever you feel like. If you want only one sentence, just write that one sentence!

I LIKE TO ASK MYSELF THREE QUESTIONS, ONE FOR EACH PARAGRAPH:

1. **What's one experience I want to tell this person?** You don't necessarily have to explain *why* you want to tell about this moment. Instead, just describe the moment itself. Example: "I hit a home run at my baseball game!"

2. **What's one big thing I wish this person could tell me right now?** Ask a question. It will keep the conversation going and make it easier for the person to pick up a pen and write back. Asking something general might get you a good, long response that could start a conversation that lasts over the course of many letters. Something fun, like "How do you feel about the ending of the Harry Potter series and why?" Then don't wait for them to ask you the same question back—answer your own question! They'll have plenty of opportunities to pick out things they want to respond to. Another option would be to ask something specific and direct. Try "What did you eat for breakfast today?" This helps to paint a picture of what their day actually looks like.

3. **What's one thing in my future that I'm excited about?** Are you going on a trip? Are you looking forward to Christmas? Write about it. This will give the recipient something to ask you about when they write back.

THE SIGN-OFF

Your sign-off is the way you end the letter, before you sign your name. These are my three favorite options for ending a letter:

1. **Think about who you are to the recipient.** Are you writing to your dad? Just write "Your daughter"! Are you a daughter who is feeling particularly hungry at that moment? Or maybe you spent the first paragraph telling your dad about the great breakfast you just finished, and the memories are making you hungry again. Jazz it up with "Your HUNGRY daughter."

2. **Another favorite way to sign off is to choose an adverb.** An adverb is a word that describes *how* you are doing something. I have

HUNGRY

Your daughter,

Truthfully,

a pretty purple journal that I carry around for ideas. I always write down lyrics and words that inspire me. I also use the journal to keep a running list of my favorite adverbs for writing letters! For example, if you're saying something in an excited or happy way, "excitedly" is the adverb to describe how you are talking. Example: "Excitedly, your friend." Or, if you're still hungry by the time you've finished the letter, write "Hungrily yours."

3. **You can also sign off with appreciation.** Troops really love knowing you care. Show them how much you respect their hard work and dedication. You can say something like "Forever appreciative" or "With gratitude."

Read over your letter once more and think of a word that describes how you are writing. Some examples are "Truthfully," "Weirdly," "Cheerfully," and "Wistfully." Sometimes it's hard to think of the perfect word on the spot, and that's when I turn to my journal so I can find the right word quickly!

Wistfully, *Cheerfully,* *ccitedly,* **With gratitude,**

You did it! You just wrote your first letter. Try one with a hero in mind, and when you're done, send it to me. I will make sure to get it in the hands of one of our troops. It will make a big difference in the life of a member of our armed forces. Ask a parent or guardian to help you go online and visit my website at **SAVANNAHSSOLDIERS.ORG** for the address to send your letter. *Make sure you always stay safe!* Please do not include any personal information, such as your last name, address, phone number, or email.

Writing letters is a really fun way to show appreciation for the people who fight for our freedom on the front lines, and to connect your world to theirs. Writing is also a great way to express yourself and learn more about what's important to you and how you can make the world around you a better place. There's a whole lot to learn about yourself by connecting with other people near and far, and a whole lot of different ways to do it. As I'm writing this book, I'm a teen singer and songwriter with my own nonprofit, but it took a lot of writing and a lot of connecting to figure out my dreams and how I could go about making them real. I want to share that journey with you.

Let's get started.

CHAPTER 2

Resilience

Chasing the Storm, Not Running from It

Resilience is the ability to recover from difficult situations or experiences. It's not a word I used a lot when I was younger, but I now see examples of resilience wherever I go. As young people in today's society, we all have to be resilient. On top of normal stuff like schoolwork and extra-curricular activities, we are also learning who we are and understanding the world around us. We are experiencing so many firsts, and so quickly. It can get . . . stressful.

One of my favorite songs to sing is the national anthem. It's a beautifully difficult song vocally, and it stands for so much. It represents freedom and is a reminder of all fallen and active-duty service members and what they've done for our country. They leave their families and homes behind, they go through difficult training, they don't get a lot of sleep, and then they are put in dangerous places. How do they do it? They are resilient.

I had to be strong when Wilson moved away. I felt alone without her. Wilson had to hold her head high because she was heartbroken that her dad was being deployed. But trying to stay positive is what keeps us strong, keeps us moving, and keeps us happy. Of course, it is okay to take some time to be sad when something bad happens. You will bounce back.

Music
- - - - - - - -

Growing up, I wanted more than anything to be a singer. In second grade, I was in chorus. After school, a group of us would get together and practice with the music teacher. I would never get the solos and was usually in the back, but I tried my best. I took every class I could find and auditioned for everything I could think of. I didn't succeed right away, and every time I failed, it took a lot of effort to dust myself off and stand back up. That wasn't easy, but I knew that if I kept at it, I would eventually do great! To this day, I believe that in order to succeed in anything, you have to really want it and be willing to keep trying, even if along the way it doesn't go exactly as planned.

When I first learned Wilson was moving away, I had just started traveling to Nashville to take songwriting lessons from a great singer-songwriter, Deborah Allen. I remember my first meeting with her like it

She stood in the storm
and when the wind
did not blow her way,

SHE ADJUSTED
HER SAILS.

— Elizabeth Edwards

was yesterday. We pulled up in front of her office on Nashville's famous Music Row. I remember feeling a little nervous but super excited! Inside the building, the walls were lined with hit records. Deb and I got straight to work. Remember that I said I would tell you more about my song for Wilson? Well, Wilson was moving, and I wanted to give her something that would make her feel happy and empowered. I brought my idea to Deb, and before I knew what was happening, we were writing one of my very first songs—"Wilson."

Looking back, I realize that writing that song was really the original bridge I built. I wrote it before I started sending letters to the soldiers in her dad's battalion. It was a song of resilience for both Wilson and me. And from there, we went on to write all those letters for her dad's unit. Together we were able to turn a sad situation into something joyful and wonderful—something that made us stronger, and made the bond between us stronger than it had been before we separated.

Now I write songs about everything. I write about soldiers who are serving overseas, but I also write as a way to express myself and deal with things going on in my own life. Of course I write about my crushes and then the fallout of crush moments. Like when a guy I liked asked another girl to homecoming . . . it's a song! Or about that boy who makes me feel like I light up the world . . . that's a song too. Writing about your challenges and obstacles can make you feel better about them. It's a way of facing your problems and organizing your emotions into something beautiful that the rest of the world can relate to.

Facing down a blank page can be overwhelming. You don't have to always write a normal letter like the one we talked about in chapter 1. Just follow your heart and write however you can. Writing poems, ideas, music, or journal entries can help you express honest and raw emotion. My heart tells me to write songs. What does yours tell you?

My Resilience Anthem

Speaking about songwriting and resilience made me think about writing a resilience anthem, which is an uplifting song that will help you get through tough times. I thought we could write one together!

The first thing you can do is write your own resilience story. Think about a really difficult time in your life. Did you cry? Ignore it? Talk to a friend? That's okay. Totally normal. Now look back at that challenging time and think about where you are today. Did you get past it? Are you feeling better? Did you survive? You did. Sometimes what feels like a million pounds of pressure on your back lasts only a short time. That is the story I'd love for you to turn into a song.

Writing music might seem hard at first, but it gets easier with practice. The best part is that there are really just a few simple rules. You can go as far as your imagination and creativity will take you. As I started to write more and more music, I made a list to help me through the process. I still use it! Here it is:

Songwriting

SHOW THE WORLD WHO YOU ARE

I: BE INSPIRED

Wilson's story first inspired me to create a song for her.

Inspiration can come from anywhere. What inspires you? Think about something that gets you excited or takes your breath away. It can be big, like your friend moving away or losing someone close to you; or it can be little, like how much you really love Pop-Tarts.

2: LYRICS

Start with a few words or a poem to kick off your lyrics.

"Thinking of him day after day . . ."

Finding the perfect *lyrics* can be the hardest part. When writing "Wilson," I thought about the words my friend used to describe what was happening with her dad. Wilson said things like "I will miss him so much when he leaves" and "My dad will be so far away." Her words really took my breath away, so I used them as a starting point. Those statements helped me come up with the first few words of the song: "Thinking of him day after day / her daddy was gone helping so far away."

3: MELODY

Experiment with chords, melodies, and rhythm. Find the perfect sound for your song.

4: RECORD

Find a way to record your ideas so that you remember them and can come back to them when you need to!

Another way to start writing a song is to just describe what you are thinking about. I do it in my purple journal, but you can use paper and a pen or get a journal of your own. Writing things down helps me to *record* my thoughts so I won't forget them. There's nothing worse than thinking of some great lyrics only to forget them later. You can use a journal or your phone, or scribble down your thoughts on a napkin. . . . Just don't forget later about the lyrics that you wrote!

5: PUT IT TOGETHER

a basic template for a song is:

VERSE
CHORUS
VERSE
CHORUS
BRIDGE
CHORUS

The next step is to take everything you've done so far and ***put it together.*** This can feel a little overwhelming, but breaking it down into smaller pieces makes it easier. (Again, remember to take it one step at a time!) I like to do this by writing the first *verse*, which helps to introduce the song. Then I go into the *chorus*, which is the part of the song that is repeated after each verse. Then another *verse*, which continues the story you started in the first verse. Then, after another *chorus*, you can add one last verse (or not!). Before singing the chorus for the last time, I like to include a *bridge*—a few words right before the final chorus that help you get ready for the end of the song. The bridge can tie up your thoughts or can tell the listener how the story ends before you go back into the *chorus*.

6: PRACTICE

Perfect your song so you can share it with friends and other writers.

Now you have to *practice* and practice to make sure you remember all the words. You don't want to write a great song and then just forget it because you didn't work on it until it was perfect!

Think about songwriting as kind of like writing a letter. In a letter, you have a salutation (greeting), the body, and then a sign-off. Writing a song is similar.

Your first verse could cover the subject: "Dear listener, here is what I am going to talk about."

The second verse can describe something that happened—maybe why you are writing the song.

And the final verse can talk about the result or the outcome of the story—sort of like your sign-off.

Your chorus is something you'll probably repeat at least three times; it will come between each of those verses, and at the end, so really think about what you most want to communicate to your audience. Usually the most important line from the chorus is the title of your song. So always think about that when writing!

HERE ARE A FEW MORE TIPS I'VE USED OVER THE YEARS:

– **Keep it simple.** Focus on one or two times in your life when you overcame an obstacle in your path. Describe the obstacle, how you dealt with it, and what you think about it now. That could be the inspiration for your song.

– **Listen to music.** Find songs that make you feel empowered and energetic. It is okay if you are having trouble creating your own original song. Just take a song you love and look closely at its lyrics. They will often inspire you to start pulling together your own phrases and words. You can definitely follow the rhyming style of the song, but make sure you change all the words to make it your own.

– **Write with a friend.** Two heads are better than one. Find some friends who like music, and write your song with them.

– **Get feedback.** You can always improve your anthem-writing skills. Share your song with people you trust, and see what they say. I bet they'll all really like it and might help you make it better.

It isn't easy to persist in the face of challenges, but if our troops can do it, then so can we. Remember, resilience is getting up when you fall down. It is continuing on even when you are afraid. It is being able to adapt to new situations while staying true to yourself. It is a quality that you already have inside you, and it can be brought out whenever you feel you need it.

A song, a letter, a journal entry, or even a drawing can help you and those around you overcome something difficult. Don't wait until things get tough—get to work now. You have it in you. Sing your resilience anthem, and sing it loud!

Now it is your turn. Before you know it, you'll be a songwriter!

CHAPTER 3

Camaraderie

Teams Build
the Dreams

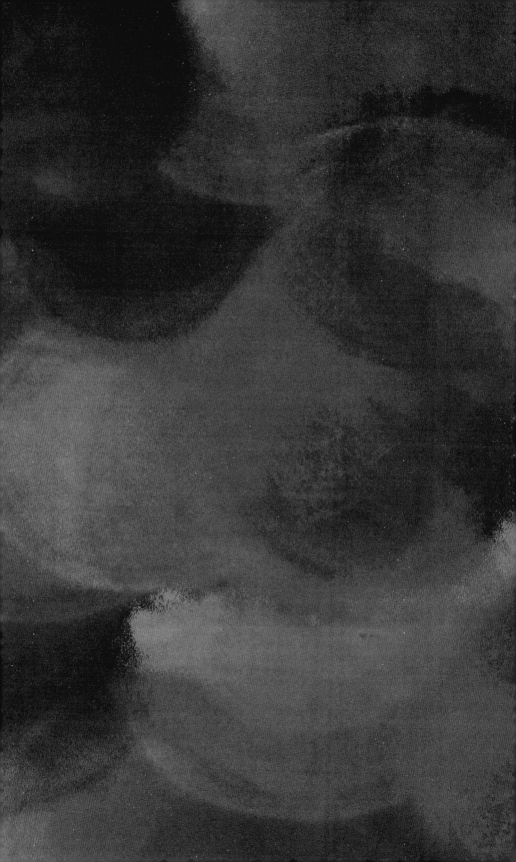

Camaraderie can mean a lot of different things, but I have always thought about it as a willingness to work as a team, no matter what. I wouldn't be here today without my friends and the people who supported me along the way! Camaraderie reminds us that no one needs to do it alone.

Being part of a team helps you to succeed, reach your goals, and connect with people around you. Your comrades keep you resilient by picking you up when you are down. Think about just how important teamwork is to our service members. Until I started writing letters, I didn't realize how much our soldiers rely on one another to protect our country and to defend our freedom here at home. When someone joins up, they become part of the biggest team in the entire world.

But you don't have to be enlisted in the military to build a team. We all need a team of our own to support our dreams and help us to live meaningful and happy lives. My mom is not just my best friend but also a really important teammate. She helped me

ALONE
we can do so little;
TOGETHER
we can do so much.

— Helen Keller

to build Savannah's Soldiers from the very beginning. She has supported my singing career by practicing with me and finding great voice coaches for me. She drove me to and from every performance, show, and singing of the national anthem at sporting events. She is so much more than just my mom. Without her, I don't know where I would be.

We all need team members to help us through the good times and the bad. I've learned that you never know who will become a part of your team. Camaraderie can be formed in the most unlikely of ways and places! As much as I knew Savannah's Soldiers was helping boost morale overseas, I didn't realize it was helping people here at home until I met Joelle. I was twelve years old at the time and was the official anthem singer for the Florida Panthers, the local professional hockey team. Singing the national anthem in front of a whole audience of hockey fans was so exciting! Joelle was an on-ice manager for the Panthers, and we shared a dressing room. We'd both show up before the game and get dressed and do our hair. We spent a lot of time together during that first season.

One day, my mom sat down and started talking to Joelle before a Panthers game. They chatted about Savannah's Soldiers and the letter-writing campaign.

Joelle thought it was pretty cool. We were surprised to learn that Joelle had had a boyfriend named Don and that they were about to get engaged before he was killed in Afghanistan while driving a Humvee over a bridge. Joelle started crying and told us that the bridge had collapsed and Don had fallen into the deep ravine. That was so hard to hear.

We kept talking, and she asked if she could help out with Savannah's Soldiers. She ended up becoming a really important team member for years. My mom told me later that she thought participating in the letter-writing campaign helped Joelle to heal. Being part of an organization and a team that focused on thanking the military must have been her way of remembering and honoring her boyfriend, who was so dedicated to his service. It also helped Joelle find friends and other people who'd been through similar difficult experiences.

Building Camaraderie

I want to help you build a team and find people who support your dreams and move you in the direction of your goals.

HERE ARE SOME OF MY FAVORITE TIPS:

- *Start with your family.* Your family is the first team you'll ever be on. Look to your mom, your dad, your brother, your sister, and whoever else is close to you.

- *No team is too small.* Don't worry if your team is just you and your best friend, or even you and your mom or dad. Just look at what started with Wilson and me!

- *Look for common interests.* Connect with people who love to do the things that you do. Are you on a sports team? In a band? Chorus? Moot court? Surrounding yourself with people who are passionate about the same things you are is how you learn and grow.

- *Don't be shy.* Build connections by getting involved and talking to people. Everyone wants to make a new friend. So when you see an opportunity to connect—take it!

- *Don't stop now.* You should always look to grow your team and add good teammates.

Camaraderie Wall

Our soldiers have taught me that teamwork happens every day and everywhere. You just can't stop it. Right after we wrote those first seven hundred letters, I remember talking to a lieutenant in the Army. My friends and I wrote letters to his battalion, and he told me the coolest thing. He said that after all the soldiers read the letters, they taped them to the wall next to one another—like wallpaper. So when they walked through the halls to get food or head back to the barracks where they slept, they could read all the letters. The lieutenant told me the hanging letters made everyone so happy. It was fun for them to read each other's letters. It made them feel camaraderie and the love from their team members at home. Reading the letters was a happy distraction and always raised team morale.

That story gave me the idea for an activity we can do together. I thought it would be really fun to create posters to be used as wallpaper that we can send to the troops to hang up in their barracks or the food halls. This is a great project to work on with someone, so grab a friend and let's get started!

1. **Grab the biggest piece of paper you can find,** or use a panel from an old cardboard box that's been lying around in your garage or basement. That is going to be your canvas.

2. **Choose any of your favorite drawing tools.** Crayons work great, but I have seen kids use paint, markers, glitter and glue, stickers, or colored pencils. Just make sure to ask an adult for help before you use anything permanent.

3. **After you've gotten your supplies together,** think about how you want to decorate your poster. You can write something fun, like a quote or maybe some lyrics from a song. Or you can just draw a picture on it—something that is super fun or cute. I've also seen kids create a collage by cutting out some pictures from a magazine and gluing them on.

ONE MORE TIP: Decorate the whole piece of cardboard and then cut it in half so that you and your friend each have your own piece. The background will match, even though you'll each add your own unique touches.

Life is really all about friendship, connecting, and surrounding yourself with people who make you happy and uplift you. No one can do it alone. Not our troops. Not our teachers. Not our leaders. Not our parents. Not our friends. And definitely not us by ourselves. We all need one another. We are built to share. You can make a difference in the world just by working to find people to support you—and returning the favor by supporting them. Build bridges by building your team!

CHAPTER 4

Courage

Heroes Face Their Fears

It's not always easy to be brave. We all have things in our lives that we are afraid of: starting at a new school, playing in a big game, performing in front of a bunch of people, or having a family member or friend get sick. Those experiences can be really scary. Wilson was scared when her dad was deployed, but I still remember how brave she and her mom and her brother were when he left. Sure, they were afraid. That's normal. But they faced their fear with great courage; in my mind, they were heroes.

That is what Eleanor Roosevelt—respected leader, hero, and First Lady of the United States—was talking about in the quotation that appears in this chapter. Her words help me understand the meaning of courage. She is saying that courage is facing fear. When you feel afraid, it's important to look at that feeling and recognize what the fear is preventing you from doing. What would you do if you didn't have fear blocking your way? Then, instead of letting the fear control you and using it as an excuse to give up, you do that exact thing. You conquer that fear.

I've learned a lot about courage from our soldiers.

Many of them have admitted to me that they get scared at times, but they have also shared with me stories of how they have fought through what has scared them. Facing your fear builds courage, but you don't have to be fighting for our country to be courageous. Courage happens every day. There is bravery in many things you do.

I was so scared when I sang the national anthem for the first time in front of a big audience at a Miami Marlins game. I was only ten. This was way before I met Joelle and sang for the Panthers. The crowd was a sea of people, all looking at me. What if I forgot a word? Was off pitch? Passed out? Oh my gosh, I was so nervous! What if I finished and they didn't cheer like I'd always seen on TV? What if I just blew it? The national anthem is one of the hardest songs to sing because everyone knows the words *and* the melody. If you mess up a line, *everyone* knows! You can't just pretend it didn't happen and expect that no one will notice.

Despite all of this, and after a couple of great pep talks from my mom, I chose to face my fear. I took a deep breath, walked to the mic at center field, and started singing. Thankfully, everything went great. And everyone stayed on their feet and cheered. It was one of the best experiences I've ever had. Since then,

I have sung the national anthem over one hundred times for teams, including the Miami Heat, the Miami Marlins, the Florida Panthers, and the Boston Red Sox, and at sporting events, like Professional Bull Riders competitions and PGA Championships—and even at military ceremonies in front of government officials!

Looking back, I realize that facing my fears opened many doors. It was such a great feeling, so I want to help you to do the same thing. It may sound scary, but I have total confidence in you.

You gain strength, courage, and confidence by every experience in which you really stop to look fear in the face.

YOU MUST DO THE THING YOU THINK YOU CANNOT DO.

—Eleanor Roosevelt

Building Courage

You don't just become courageous over-night. It happens little by little, in any small moment when you feel fear and decide to just move forward. Standing up to a bully is a moment of courage. Asking your crush to the school dance takes courage too. Sometimes you might face the same fear again and again. Courage is sticking with it even though it might not be easy. There are fears that take years to overcome, but when you do, it is worth it!

HERE ARE SOME WAYS I DEAL WITH MY FEARS:

- *Take deep breaths.* I'm not afraid of performing anymore, but I still get nervous just before I go onstage. Now I take deep breaths, in through my nose and out through my mouth. Deep breaths help to slow my heart rate and give me a chance to focus and center my thoughts so that I can perform to the best of my ability.

- **Don't do it alone.** Camaraderie. Make sure you have your friends or your team by your side. Soldiers always tell me it helps to know there are people just like them dealing with the same fears. Then they can work together as one unit to overcome anything.

- **Practice.** Being prepared will help you erase any doubt in your mind. Soldiers practice drills, mission plans, and objectives. I write down all my speeches before I give them, and I practice my songs until they are perfect.

- **Get inspired.** Courage is everywhere. It is in our local heroes, like firefighters and police officers. It is in a student who tries out for a sports team or the school play. There is courage in going to a new school. Doing something out of your comfort zone. Standing up for something you believe in. If you need a little help finding your own courage, get inspired by reading books about courageous people, watching movies about bravery, or talking to your teammates. You'll learn a lot about how those people found their inner strength.

I know it is not always easy to feel courageous, especially when you are dealing with something that is pretty scary. But you aren't in this alone, and taking deep breaths, practicing, finding inspiration, and reaching out to other people who might feel the same way will absolutely help you fight through your fears, big and little.

Brave Bands

THINGS YOU WILL NEED FOR THIS ACTIVITY:

- Scissors
- Glue stick or transparent tape
- Paper
- Pens
- Crayons

It is important to remind yourself that you are brave and courageous and you can face all your fears, so I want to help you always have something close by.

I call them Brave Bands. Take a moment and write out a few reasons why you are brave. You could reference something courageous you did, a skill you have, or a trait that describes you.

I DID A FEW, AND HERE IS WHAT I CAME UP WITH:

I don't let stage fright stop me from pursuing my dreams.

I always try to help people who need it.

I see what our soldiers experience.

I tried something new today.

I worked hard to get over my fears.

I did things that others thought I couldn't.

Pick your favorite message you wrote on paper, and then cut it out and glue the ends together around your wrist. Once you are done, you can wear your Brave Band and show it off to your friends! If you feel scared or nervous about something, just look at your Brave Band for a reminder that you can do it. If you want to remind yourself of something secret, you can wear the band inside out, with the words against your skin.

Here are some empowering words to help get you writing!

ADVENTUROUS HOPEFUL

AMAZING INNOVATIVE

BRAVE INSPIRING

BRILLIANT INTELLIGENT

CONFIDENT LEADER

COURAGEOUS ORGANIZED

DETERMINED PATIENT

DRIVEN POSITIVE

EXCEPTIONAL POWERFUL

FABULOUS RESILIENT

FOCUSED STRONG

FREE TALENTED

HAPPY UNIQUE

YOU CAN PUT BRAVE BANDS ALMOST ANYWHERE, NOT JUST ON YOUR WRIST. HERE ARE SOME IDEAS:

— Loop your Brave Band around a backpack strap.

— Place your Brave Band inside a clear phone case and then put the case on your phone.

— Hang it on your fridge with magnets.

— Put it on the wall in your room.

— Stick it to the inside of your locker at school.

You can make Brave Bands for friends and family members or even slip one in a letter with a special message for a service member. Everyone needs a reminder about why they can get through anything. Share the bravery!

You are a hero every single time you face your fears. No matter how big or how small they are, you should celebrate overcoming something you are afraid of.

I encourage you to try something new today! If you were waiting for a sign that you should overcome something, let this be it.

CHAPTER 5

Preparation

Be Ready to Deliver an Amazing Performance

Have you ever worked really hard on a project? Or stayed up late studying for a test? Ever practice your dance routine or basketball shot for hours on end? You might have even worked hard practicing for your school's talent show or writing a book report. Every time you put in the effort to do a great job, you were preparing to deliver a great performance!

Preparation and practice are amazingly important difference makers. In each of these examples, preparation might be the difference between getting an A on your book project, passing your test, nailing your dance routine, hitting a game-winning jump shot, or doing a fantastic job in front of an audience. No matter how big the challenge in front of you might seem, you will be able to handle it more easily if you prepare for it. Then you will be in a good spot to succeed and wow your teachers, classmates, friends, parents, or even your entire school.

This chapter includes a quotation from Benjamin Franklin, one of the founders of America and a gifted inventor. His words remind us that if you want to succeed in anything you do, you have to work hard, practice, and be prepared for it. Otherwise, you are really just leaving things up to luck. The most successful people in the world aren't successful by chance. They know that luck in itself isn't reliable! The trick is minimizing the chance for things to go wrong. How do you do this? Practice!

Setting a high standard for yourself helps you to be a better person for *you*. You're letting *yourself* down if you blow off preseason training and show up on the first day of practice out of shape, or if you don't do a homework assignment because you wanted to watch television.

But I've also learned that practice isn't just something you do for yourself; it is also for everyone around you. Being prepared is a way of showing respect to your teammates and friends. You let your whole team down if you are the only one who shows up without a jersey for the big game or if you forget the lyrics or sing off-key at an important concert.

Practice and preparation are real game changers. They can make a huge difference in your life and the lives of those around you. Because I got to sing the national anthem for a bunch of different professional sports teams in Florida, I was able to observe just how much the teams practice and how hard they prepare before every single game. It was amazing to see the work that goes into the process. I know the same is true for our troops. They go through months of training and preparation before they are deployed. Hard work, dedication, and practice are part of their everyday recipe for success. They practice daily and prepare for each mission, no matter how big or small.

I get that it might feel like a chore sometimes, but the people around you can sense the care and love you put into your work. People can tell when you just slap something together or don't give it your all. You can't hide it. Loving and valuing the details gives something special and extra to whatever you are performing or creating. The world around you will notice!

PRACTICE ISN'T JUST SOMETHING YOU DO FOR YOURSELF; IT IS ALSO FOR EVERYONE AROUND YOU.

I practice for hours and hours before every one of my performances. It took years of effort to significantly improve at singing, songwriting, playing the guitar, dancing, and everything else I really love to do. None of that happened in just a few days or with only a little bit of practice. It's hard to see in the beginning, but that effort will make a huge difference in the long run. I don't regret it at all and am thankful I learned the value of practice very early in my life.

By failing
to prepare,
you prepare
to fail.
—Benjamin Franklin

I was ten years old when I first started learning how to play the guitar. I took lessons with a teacher named Adam. I was super confused at first because, to be totally honest, I expected it to be easy. It looked so easy when artists played onstage! To my surprise, it was quite difficult to press down hard enough on the strings to make a pretty sound. It just wasn't natural and felt weird. I got frustrated often and almost quit on a few occasions. But Adam kept motivating me to work hard at it, and we would practice and practice and practice. He wouldn't let me quit. Adam made it seem fun, and he challenged me to be my best.

Eventually I learned every chord to one of my first original songs, "Do You Believe?" I remember coming home from a lesson with Adam and telling my parents and younger sister that I wanted to play something for them. I played the song for them, and they were so proud of me. Looking back, I recall that as one of the first times I saw that practice pays off. I had worked so hard to learn to play the guitar, and there I was in our living room, playing a whole song for my family! Now I play the guitar all the time. It is much easier and almost feels like second nature to me!

Learning to play the guitar was one of my first lessons in the power of preparation. It was hard work, but it was also totally worth it. That's really the cool part of preparing for anything you do—you put in the effort in the beginning but get rewarded at the end. Seeing how something hard can become much easier keeps me focused on always preparing, whether it is for a guitar lesson with my teacher or for something much bigger, like performing in front of the employees of a huge company like Walmart.

I had the chance to spread the message about Savannah's Soldiers on the *Today* show, and after it aired, Walmart's management asked if I would speak at the company's Veterans Day ceremony in Bentonville, Arkansas, where Walmart is based. I had done some public speaking, but nothing that big. I knew this would be an incredible opportunity. I had to get to work. I started to prepare and practice a speech that would be broadcast to all the Walmart and Sam's Club employees in America.

Even though I was nervous, I was prepared and knew my stuff. Before I went onstage at the Walmart headquarters in Arkansas, I sat in a large conference area, waiting to be called up. The actor Jon Voight walked into the room. I couldn't believe it. His daughter is Angelina Jolie, and I had just watched her in *Maleficent*! I walked onstage when it was my turn, and the color guard began presenting the flags. I took my place and started to sing the national anthem. When I was done, everyone in the room clapped for me! I gave the speech I had prepared, and it ended in a standing ovation. I felt like I had nailed it. Looking back, I know it was easy only because I was prepared.

Practice makes perfect, whether it's just you and your guitar, or you in front of your whole family!

Practice Is Perfectly Fun

So let's talk about how we can make practice really fun. Here are some things I have noticed that turn practice and preparation into a party!

1. **Don't do it alone.** My number one way to make preparation and practice fun is by doing it with a friend or a group. You get to spend quality time with the people you love to be around, and you learn something new in the process. I've always preferred studying for tests with a friend and making flash cards and quizzing each other. That approach makes studying much easier. Your friends, loved ones, and teachers will also keep you motivated to never stop preparing along the way.

2. **Take breaks and relax.** Preparation is so important that you really have to be focused when you do it. It is easy to get distracted at times; that's why I always take breaks and don't leave my preparation to the last minute. Some days are better than others, and it is okay

to need time off to recharge and reenergize. Sometimes I like to get a snack, watch a quick television show, text with some friends, check my Facebook, or take my dog for a walk.

3. **Do things you love.** It really doesn't even feel like practice when you are doing something you enjoy. Whenever I start to prepare for a speaking engagement or presentation, I get excited because I know how much fun it is to be onstage singing and speaking in front of an audience. It makes preparing for the moment that much better, since there is a huge payoff at the end. It is exciting to prepare and send hundreds of letters to service members—I imagine how they'll feel once they receive them. That makes it super easy to put in the long hours it takes to write, review, decorate, address, and deliver the letters to the post office.

4. **Use fun technology.** When I started writing this book, I got an iPad Pro with an Apple Pencil as a gift. I would use it to edit and work through different ideas. I could brainstorm by doodling and drawing pictures, which made the work a lot more fun. When I sing, I also love to use my phone to record songs and short

videos of me singing. It is really cool to watch yourself and listen to your voice while practicing. I have also used technology such as Skype to "visit" schools I may have been too busy to speak at in person. Adding in technology can really spice up your preparation.

Remember, it doesn't matter whether you are writing a letter to the troops or preparing for a big speech, project, or interview; it is always important to practice. Preparation and practice ensure that you'll succeed and that you won't be as nervous when it is showtime or game time. Because you've done it before, you'll have the confidence that you can do it again and again.

Polishing Your Letters

To make sure you write the best letters that you can, you have to take some time to review them before mailing them. Editing is a form of practice because you double-check your work to see that you are putting your best foot forward at all times. Sure, it's easy to just finish your letter, stuff it into an envelope, and send it off. But I bet you wouldn't do that before turning in a book report, a research paper, or an essay! Editing your work shows that you really care and have put in time and energy to create something special. Here are ways you can prepare your letter for takeoff:

Edit the Letter

I ALWAYS FOLLOW SIX STEPS WHEN EDITING MY LETTERS.

1. Read it over once for grammar and spelling mistakes.

2. If I have to make a lot of changes, I copy it onto fresh paper so there aren't editing scribbles all over the place.

3. Read it again with an eye for the story. I always ask myself this question: Did I forget an important detail?

4. Don't be afraid to delete something entirely and start over.

5. Read it out loud. If something sounds weird coming out of your mouth, it will probably sound weird to your reader.

6. Keep an eye out for repetition. Are you repeating certain words a lot? Replace them with a similar word or phrase that describes what you mean.

Editing doesn't mean the original wasn't great—it's an opportunity to make your letter even better!

Once you're happy with the content of your letter, it's time to decorate! This is the most fun part. Add stickers, draw, or paint! You can also decorate certain words in your letter by putting designs around them. The sky's the limit when it comes to creativity!

Finally, double-check our address. Send your letters to Savannah's Soldiers, and we will take care of the rest. You can put them in an envelope or a box, depending on how many you have. We will be sure to get them to a battalion in need!

OUR ADDRESS IS ALWAYS AVAILABLE AT

SAVANNAHSSOLDIERS.ORG

CHAPTER 6

Creativity

Brushstrokes on the Canvas of Life

Creativity can come in many shapes and sizes. Even though we have all felt creative at one time or another, creativity isn't always easy to describe. Some people think that being creative means they have to be an artist, an actor, maybe even a musician or an author. I disagree. I think creativity is a mindset that can help you to solve everyday problems and have fun doing it. Sometimes creativity is taking risks and breaking the rules. Other times it is putting your head together with a friend to overcome a challenge. It's a powerful and important skill that's already inside of us. We just have to find a way to show it to the world.

I look at creativity as a three-step process. The first step is to think about something, like a solution to a problem, or a way to connect to the world around you, or just a way of seeing things differently than other people might. After you've thought about things or daydreamed for a while, the next step is to write some of your thoughts down. Finally, you can turn your thoughts into reality by planning them out a little bit, asking questions, and talking about your ideas with other people.

STEP 1: THINK, DAYDREAM, AND IMAGINE.

STEP 2: JOT DOWN ALL YOUR IDEAS.

STEP 3: TURN YOUR THOUGHTS INTO A REALITY.

Daydreaming is the key to being creative. In fact, once you start daydreaming, you're already well on your way to being creative! Give yourself time and space to let your mind wander to far-off places. Dream about food you like to eat, something you've read recently, or some other things that seem fun and exciting. I always love to go outside and sit on the porch with my dogs and look out at the trees and grass. Sometimes I close my eyes and imagine sitting on a beautiful beach and staring out at the blue ocean. It introduces creative energy and helps me think outside the box. I have friends who like to go for walks to get creative, or jump in a pool, or go to the movies, or listen to some music. There are so many ways to help your mind come up with unique and cool ideas.

Moving from thoughts to action is like crossing a bridge. Sometimes it is a short bridge, and other times a long one. But you just have to cross it. It can feel a little overwhelming to cross the bridge from thoughts to action, but one of my favorite ways to do it is by writing down my thoughts in my purple journal. Sometimes I make a list; other times I write a paragraph describing what I'm thinking. I've even drawn pictures to help.

After I do that, I read through my journal and try to figure out how to turn my thoughts into something real. When it comes to writing songs, I might jot down some lyrics. I then start humming a melody or saying the words out loud to help me piece them together. I used this process when I wrote "Wilson." The point is that it helps to get the thoughts down on paper so you can see them and really get inspired by them.

THE CREATIVE PROCESS ISN'T COMPLETE UNTIL WE PUT OUR THOUGHTS INTO ACTION.

You can't use up

The more you use,

THE MORE YOU HAVE.

—Maya Angelou

Otherwise they are just hopes and dreams, which are good but won't help to change the world. So look at *thinking* as the part of creativity that is within you, and *action* as the part that other people can see when you bring it to life. One without the other is like a guitar without strings—it won't make any noise.

I remember when we were first brainstorming ideas to expand Savannah's Soldiers and recruit even more kids to write letters. I would stay up in bed every single night, and my mind would wander as I tried to think of new and creative ways to expand our letter-writing campaign. We needed to recruit a *lot* of kids, fast, and in an inexpensive way.

I finally came up with a great idea. At all the sporting events I'd been going to, I had noticed vendors and companies with booths set up inside the arenas. They'd give away new products or talk about their businesses with people passing by. They always looked really inviting while they were smiling and interacting with the people at the game. I thought we could do the same thing, but instead of offering or discussing products, we'd encourage kids to write letters. So I pulled out my journal and started to make a list of the steps I thought we'd have to take to set up a booth of our own. I had never done anything like that before, so I asked the vendors and companies already at the events how they had gotten into the arena in the first place. They were very helpful, and I took plenty of notes. Eventually I had a great plan in place.

First, we scheduled a meeting with the Miami Marlins baseball team. The Marlins already had a night when they celebrate veterans and service members: "Military Mondays." They thought our booth would be a natural fit and agreed to give us a spot in the plaza level right above home plate to set up our letter-writing table! This was exciting because *tons* of baseball fans come to the Military Monday games, so we knew that there would be plenty of people interested in stopping to write.

There are always many booths at the games promoting different things. I wanted to come up with a way for ours to stand out so little kids would want to approach the booth and write a letter during the game. To do that, we filled our table with colors, crayons, markers, stickers, American flags, and other art materials to get everyone excited and draw them in. We would have kid volunteers who were already part of the letter-writing campaign help to set up the booth and work it before and after the games.

The best part was that we got a bunch of military members in uniform to stay at the booth and talk to the event-goers as they walked by. Everyone wanted to write a letter when they saw what we were doing!

They were also excited to do some art and have some fun with Savannah's Soldiers. After getting such a positive reaction during the Marlins games, we went on to do the same thing through partnerships with the Miami Heat, Florida Panthers, Professional Golfers Association, Professional Bull Riders, and many more organizations. It was awesome!

YOU CAN USE CREATIVITY TO DO ALMOST ANYTHING, EVEN WRITE A LETTER TO A MILITARY MEMBER.

Here is what a lot of Savannah's Soldiers do: They imagine what type of situation the soldier is in and think about what he or she might like to hear from them. Even though the letter writers might have never met the service members who will read their letters, they like to ask questions, since it gets the creative juices going. Looking at magazines or newspaper pictures can help them to imagine some of the things that might interest the soldiers they are writing to. After that, they start to organize their ideas and put them in a letter format, like the one we went over in chapter 1!

If it weren't for creativity, I am pretty sure I would still be sitting at my kitchen table, writing every one of these letters by myself. Creativity can change the world. It can help you find out what you're good at and what you love to do. I know just how powerful it can be, and I think it is important that you always try to use your imagination and let your curiosity shine through. You'll be able to generate new ideas, overcome obstacles, focus on problems, and find solutions. That can open up your mind and give you some pretty cool perspectives on the world around you. Asking questions will also help you use your creative mind and have fun with the activity in this chapter—creating your own superhero.

Creating Your Own Superhero

I work with superheroes every day—the men and women who serve in our military. We see how much of themselves they pour into their service. I think they are the real-life superheroes. Now let's use that as inspiration and really let our imaginations fly. We can do this by creating our own superhero! This activity will help you let your mind wander and come up with wild, unpredictable ideas. Then we will put pen to paper and make those imaginative daydreams come to life.

Grab some pencils or markers and a piece of paper. A key to being creative is giving yourself time, so don't rush. Take as much time as you need to create your superhero.

START BY THINKING ABOUT THE ANSWERS TO THESE QUESTIONS:

- What kind of superpower does your superhero have? Can your superhero fly and leap over tall buildings like Superman? Is she really strong like Wonder Woman? Does your superhero have lots of cool gadgets like Batman's?

- What is your superhero's name?

- Does your superhero have a symbol or logo? (Batman's is a bat symbol, and Superman has a big "S" on his chest.) What is it?

- Does your superhero have a signature phrase or mantra?

- What colors does your superhero wear? Why?

- Did anyone you know inspire your superhero? Why?

Once you have a clear picture of your superhero in your mind, you can start drawing your character. Use a pencil at first so you can make as many changes as you want. Then break out the markers or pencils and color in as much as you want! Make sure to also include your superhero's powers.

So what should you do with your newly created superhero? If you know someone who is in need of a superhero, send your drawing to them. Or if someone you know inspired your superhero, make sure you tell them your superhero is based on them and send them a picture. At Savannah's Soldiers, we get a ton of superhero drawings based on the real heroes deployed overseas! Whether you are creating a letter-writing campaign or choosing the color of the tights your superhero will wear, your imagination and your creativity are key skills to help you reach any goal or overcome any challenge in front of you.

CHAPTER 7

Confidence

....

Taking Advantage of Your Window of Opportunity

....

Inspiration. Resilience. Camaraderie. Bravery. Preparation. Creativity. Each of these traits helps you to not only write letters or sing a song but also find your own sense of happiness. These are the meaningful characteristics that are inside you.

But confidence is a little different. Confidence helps you to inspire others, to become more resilient, to build camaraderie, to feel brave, to prepare, and to show the world how creative you can be. Confidence is the quality that unleashes all of your other exceptional qualities for the entire world to see. It is a feeling that you can accomplish anything you want to. It is a sense of self-assurance that comes from the self-appreciation of your abilities. Confidence helps you to live a better life by being willing to connect with people around you.

If you watch superhero movies, the superheroes are always confident by the end because they feel assured of their superpowers and strength. Their confidence actually *becomes* one of their superpowers. If you are confident, you'll just know that you've got it and won't be afraid to show it off. You'll be much more willing to put yourself out there, and take risks and seize opportunities—all because you aren't scared to fail or fall short of your goals.

I try to wear my confidence every day, even when I am nervous or scared. When I was about thirteen, right after we started Savannah's Soldiers, my mom and I were having breakfast at a restaurant in New York City on a winter day. I remember being excited because we were planning to hop around town and go shopping that day, and I LOVE shopping. My mom looked over at another table and then looked at me with big eyes. She said, "That's Larry King sitting over there." I couldn't believe it. I knew exactly who he was, since my mom always watched his show, *Larry King Live*.

Well, we finished our breakfast and left the restaurant to go to a big toy store to buy some Christmas presents. We started walking in the snow and made it about six blocks before I thought, "Maybe I should've spoken to Larry." He had been only a few tables away from me. What if he could put me on his show? I knew he was a huge influencer, and so I looked at my mom and said, "We have to go back and talk to Larry King right now."

I tried to convince her that I might not ever get

The most beautiful thing
you can wear is confidence.
— Blake Lively

this opportunity again. She finally agreed to turn around! We trekked through the snow once again, and I walked back into the restaurant. I went right up to him and said, "I have this idea, and I think I can change the world. I would like your help." He looked at me and responded, "Tell me about it." Larry was sitting by himself, and he invited me to sit down across from him. I waved my mom over and introduced her, and she sat with us. I started to talk about being on the *Today* show and about Savannah's Soldiers. When I was done, he gave me the info for his assistant and said, "Well, let's get you on my show!"

I did get on his show, and it ended up being one of the most rewarding but difficult interviews I've ever done. He didn't go easy on me or cut any breaks for this thirteen-year-old! He asked very tough questions, trying to determine how someone as young as I was could teach other kids about the military, about war, and about 9/11. I did my best to answer his questions and thought I did a pretty good job, especially since I had

Confide
TO UNLOCKIN
Finding TRU
and REACHIN

ce IS KEY

connection,

Happiness,

YOUR Goals.

made sure to prepare and practice ahead of time. All my preparation and studying beforehand paid off, and I felt really confident.

We had a lot more kids sign up to write letters after I appeared on *Larry King Live.* It was a huge success. Sure, it was scary to walk right up to Larry King at a restaurant in Times Square. I didn't even do it the first time I had the chance. It took six blocks of walking in the snow in New York City for me to decide that it'd be a good idea to turn around. It wasn't easy to sit across from him and answer his tough interview questions on his show, but confidence is what helped me through it. Some people are just naturally confident, but the rest of us need a little help. That is totally normal.

In the second chapter, we learned that being resilient helps to build confidence; looking back at how you dealt with hurdles reminds you that you are capable of overcoming obstacles and recovering from a challenge. Feeling brave or courageous definitely helps your confidence level because you aren't scared to face your fears head-on.

And in the third chapter, we discussed that having the support and camaraderie of your friends and family can help you to feel even more confident. I've overcome some of my biggest fears and challenges just by having my friends by my side. (That's why you never go to haunted houses by yourself!)

In the fifth chapter, we talked about how preparation makes you feel confident that you'll do a great job. Don't forget that practicing can have a huge impact when it comes to confidence.

There's no doubt you'll feel confident if you are resilient, are supported by friends and family, and practice again and again. If you remember these things, your confidence will take you places that you never imagined you could go!

Positive-Thought Journaling

I think it is common for us to wonder how we can confidently share our thoughts and feelings with others. Since I spend a lot of time speaking in classroom settings, I have noticed that some kids don't participate in class because they don't feel what they have to say is smart or important. That's certainly not the case. They just need to up their confidence level. If you use your mind, you'll always have creative things to share.

This all starts with focusing on positive self-talk. That means you don't say things like "I'm terrible at signing" or "I'm not going to pass this test or get good grades" or even "I'm never going to amount to anything." These are all confidence killers, and we want to build confidence.

When I'm feeling negative, I go back to my purple journal and write down positive thoughts.

HERE ARE SOME GOOD PLACES TO START:

— List some things you like about yourself.

— Describe times when you succeeded or accomplished a goal, and detail how you did it.

— List all the people who love you and have your back. What would they say to cheer you up?

— Write down the lessons you learned when you didn't quite reach your goals. These will help you to learn from your mistakes (which are totally normal and okay to make).

— Pretend the whole world is a stage and you are auditioning. In your journal, write down how you can best prepare for your performance!

— Keep singing. Include some of your favorite inspirational quotes and lyrics from songs.

— Use some of these sentence prompts to get the positive thoughts flowing:

I'm proud of . . .

In school, I am good at . . .

I was really happy when . . .

I like myself because . . .

I knew I took a big step after . . .

One of my biggest accomplishments is . . .

I overcame a challenge when I . . .

I was brave when . . .

One of my favorite things to do is . . .

I helped a friend by . . .

— Write down affirmations. Affirmations start with the word "I." They are positive, short, and specific. Here are some examples:

I am friendly.

I am helpful.

I am loved.

I am caring and loving to my friends and family.

I am exactly where I want to be.

I can solve any problem in my path.

I enjoy trying new things.

I like meeting new people.

I have positive thoughts.

I enjoy learning.

I like singing, dancing, and playing around with my friends.

I am strong, inside and out.

I am comfortable with who I am.

I am beautiful.
I am handsome.
I am totally awesome.
I am full of energy.

I have dreams and I believe in them.

I am confident in who I am.

I have the courage to be myself.

I appreciate a challenge.

I am strong.
I am brave.
I am happy . . . really happy.

Positive-thought journaling is an easy and powerful way to build up your confidence and remind you exactly why you should be confident in the first place.

Whether you're walking up to a celebrity in a restaurant, trying something that scares you, introducing yourself to a new friend, or just knowing you can dream big, confidence is key to unlocking connection, finding true happiness, and reaching your goals.

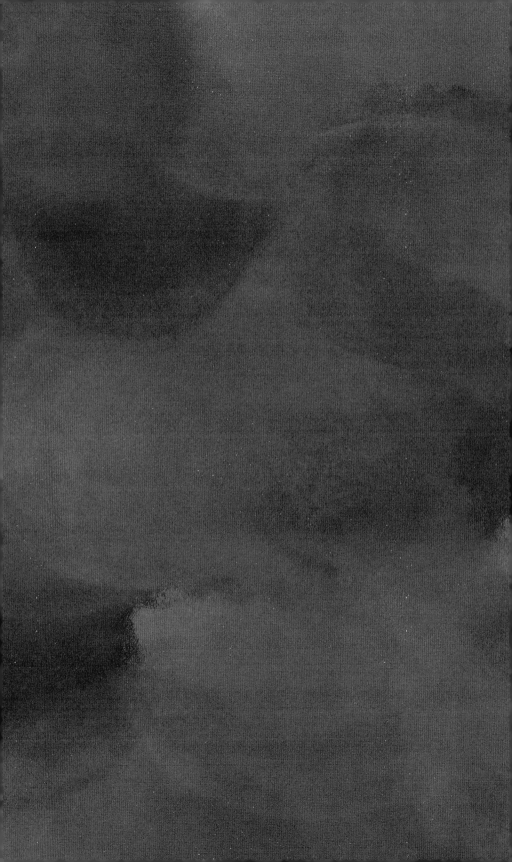

CHAPTER 8

Flexibility

Thinking on Your Feet

The road between "here" and "there" isn't always an easy one to follow. Sometimes it can be winding, bumpy, and difficult. You can prepare and practice as much as humanly possible, but you can't predict every setback along the way. You have to be willing to adjust to situations that pop up suddenly and are out of your control.

When I say "flexibility," I don't mean stretching and yoga. Flexibility is about adapting in the moment and going with the flow. If you can learn how to adjust to different situations and experiences, I am confident that you'll be able to accomplish almost anything.

To truly be flexible, you have to be willing to change things and compromise in the moment. I learned that lesson firsthand with Camplified, which is a summer camp concert tour that turns camps across the nation into music festivals. Camplified booked me as one of the main acts to travel the country and perform in front of thousands of kids at massive summer camps. My band and I had performed at a few camps and eventually made it to Camp Blue Ridge, right outside Atlanta, Georgia. It was me and a few other bands, including a pretty popular rock band.

Each band spent the day setting up for the event, and we were about to perform in a big outdoor pavilion. The bands were so excited because it was a major production with sound, lights, and a big stage. But then disaster hit. We heard thunder and saw lightning, and the skies opened up. The entire audience was led out of the pavilion and squished into the cafeteria to wait out the storm. We threw tarps over the sound equipment and followed everyone inside and away from the dangerous weather. We waited and waited and waited. While my band and I were hanging in the cafeteria, the other bands packed up their stuff and loaded it into the trucks, since they couldn't perform in the terrible weather and it was getting late.

We watched the bands leave, one by one, until finally we were the last act left sitting there. The campers were so disappointed; they had been looking forward to the concert for a while. The camp had advertised the concert for weeks, and the campers had made posters and learned the songs all before we had even gotten there! We couldn't leave the kids without a show, but the weather was still horrible. So I had my musicians change to acoustic instruments. We ran outside in the rain and got as many instruments as we could from the packed-up trucks. We had an acoustic bass and guitar and a drum set.

There was a cajón too, which is like a mini drum that you sit on and play with your hands. Completely drenched, we walked back into the cafeteria, and the kids started clapping for us.

There was a little stage, and we had the entire audience sit on the floor around it. We plugged in as many amps and mics as we could, and we played a full forty-five-minute set. We stayed after and signed autographs for hours. It was completely wild, and the campers loved it.

Ultimately it was a really good performance, but it almost didn't happen. Even though we didn't have an official plan B when we arrived at Blue Ridge, we were flexible and adjusted in the moment so that we could give the audience an awesome time. We rocked the camp. It was so much fun.

What's Your Plan B?

Flexibility can change your life. It can help you make new friends, adapt to a new school, or deal with sad events, like a friend moving away or a parent being deployed.

Flexibility helps to open up your mind and heart to make things easier in the long run.

I want you to have a plan B in everything you do. You might be auditioning for the lead role in *Rent* or competing for a spot on the junior varsity soccer team. Maybe you're trying out for the debate squad or running for class president at your high school. You might just want to get a part-time job at a new boutique in town. These are all your plan A's, and it's good to have goals and to work hard to reach them. But what if you fall just a little short? That doesn't mean you are a failure or should just quit. Even Michael Jordan, one of the best basketball players of all time, didn't make his high school basketball team at first! His plan B was to work hard and get better so he'd never miss the cut again. It worked out for him in the end, obviously!

Since I love performing, I am always auditioning for shows, musicals, and plays. As you can imagine, there is a lot of competition for certain roles. Everyone wants to be Elle Woods or the lead character in *Peter Pan* or *Grease.* But only one person gets the role. I am always a little disappointed if I don't get the part, but that's totally normal. I do my best to stay resilient, and I keep trying until I succeed. You win some and you lose many more.

There is a popular expression: When God closes a door, he often opens a window. But how do you look for the window?

THERE'S *ALWAYS* ANOTHER PATH YOU CAN TAKE TO REACH YOUR GOAL AS LONG AS YOU STAY DETERMINED WHEN THINGS GET CHALLENGING.

Let's draw out some options to help you be more flexible in your life! On the following pages is a menu I created to map out my plan B. It has categories like hobbies, goals, dreams, friendships, family, job, and after-school activities. I filled in all the spaces with my own answers. I want to help you do the same. So grab a piece of paper and sketch out a menu of your own. Draw in a bunch of boxes like I did in my example, and then label the boxes at the top. List your favorites under each one. This will help you to recognize just how many things you love and how many options are available to you! Seeing all these different opportunities should help you to be flexible and realize that if you don't get your first choice, there are lots of other exciting prospects available to you.

THINGS I LOVE

Singing • Guitar • Dancing
Acting • Songwriting

GOALS

Perform often • Become a better guitarist

Send **ONE MILLION LETTERS** to military member

Be more like my mom • Do well in school

DREAMS

Sell out Madison Square Garden

Share my music • Travel the worl

COMRADES

My amazing little sister, Sierra

My mom, aka my number one supporter

My dad • My grandparents • My friends

JOBS

Singer • Writer • Actor

PRACTICE TIME

Guitar • Vocal lessons

Recording • Songwriting sessions

HOW WILL I GET THERE?

Working hard • Practicing

Learning from my teachers

Working with friends • Preparing

My Plan B

When it comes to living our lives, things can unexpectedly change, even day to day. Being flexible and willing to adapt is really where it's at. It keeps you on your path and prevents the bumps in the road from becoming mountains that can get in your way.

Intelligence is the ability to adapt to change.

— Stephen Hawking

CHAPTER 9

Compassion

Building Lasting
Connections

I will never forget how it felt to sit on the playground and listen to my friend Wilson pour her heart out to me about her dad's deployment. It was so sad, and she was really hurting inside. I remember looking right into her eyes and being able to feel her sadness and pain. I knew she was going through something hard and was going to miss her dad more than anything. We were so close and such good friends. I wanted to do something to make her feel better. I wanted to help my best friend. As you know, my response was to write a song to show her just how much I cared. I hoped it would make her feel better. And just maybe it would help her a little bit to get through the tough times of not only missing her dad but also leaving her school and her friends.

When you think about compassion, you might think about words like "sympathy," "concern," "care," "kindness," and "love." In one way or another, compassion is all of those things. Some people think about caring for others as being supportive toward people only during the tough times in their lives. But these acts of kindness should be an everyday choice that shows we are all in this together. You might want to celebrate with a friend who got good grades, or get excited about a friend who made the softball team. We should always help each other out, no matter what. I know I need compassion, and I try to show it to my friends, to my family, and even to strangers every day.

My favorite part about being compassionate is not just how it helps other people feel better, but also how it makes me feel. It makes me happy when I know I am there for someone.

I started Savannah's Soldiers because I knew a little bit of caring could go a long way. I was also confident that many of my friends felt the same way and were looking to positively impact the world. I wanted to spread that feeling, so I recruited people to help me send some love and kindness across the world.

Treat people as if they were what they ought to be, and you help them to become what they are capable of being.

— Johann Wolfgang von Goethe

When you write a letter to a soldier, you really take a moment to put yourself in their shoes. And as you close your eyes and think about what to write, you can imagine how they feel, what they are experiencing, and maybe even how much they miss their loved ones. Think about what you'd want someone to say to you to help make you feel supported, loved, and confident.

Compassion in Your Community

I have learned that it is really easy to be compassionate. Some people are just born that way and are always thinking about others in everything they do. But for most of us, it is simply caring for humanity, being aware of people around us, and finding ways to help them out. To do that, I came up with a list of things you can do in your local community on a daily basis. They are super easy, and they might take only a few seconds, but each one spreads compassion throughout the world. Your challenge? Pick five of these acts to do this week!

Turn Compassion into Action

- Hold the door for someone, even if you don't know them.

- Help your neighbor keep up their lawn by shoveling snow in the winter (unless you live in Florida, like I did), raking leaves in the fall, and pulling weeds in the summer.

THANK YOU!

- Say thank you whenever someone does something kind for you.

- Volunteer at an animal shelter.

- Send a letter to someone in the military (one of my favorites!).

- Help an elderly person to their car.

- Pick up something that someone might have dropped, and deliver it to the lost and found.

- Help carry someone's groceries home.

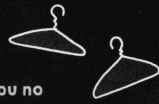

- Donate clothes you no longer wear.

- Bake cookies or brownies for your local firefighters or police officers.

- **Leave a nice note on someone's car.**

- Make dinner or pick up a meal for a friend whose relative passed away.

- **Hold the elevator, even if you are in a rush.**

- Offer someone your seat on the bus or train.

- Help your brother or sister do their homework or their chores.

- **Clear the table after you're done eating dinner.**

- Help your mom or dad make lunch or breakfast on the weekend.

- Compliment someone. Let them know you like their jacket or shoes.

— Help teachers clean up their classrooms.

— **Paint or draw a picture for someone.**

— Eat lunch with someone who usually eats alone at school.

— Volunteer for a charity in your community.

— Forgive your friends or family when they upset you.

— Post a nice comment on your friend's Facebook or Instagram page.

These actions are so small and really easy to do, but they can make a huge difference in someone's day. If you need a little inspiration, don't hesitate to look at my list or ask a friend or an adult for help. Pick a few things and check them off once you do them. You can even add to the list! I am always thinking about spreading compassion to my friends, family, and even strangers. Whenever I come up with a fun way to do so, I write it down in my purple journal.

The best part about being compassionate is that you can see its effects almost immediately. How many times have you smiled at someone and they've smiled right back? Or maybe you posted a positive message to a friend and they posted one right back? How about holding the elevator for someone? I'm sure they thanked you and showed their appreciation.

Compassion spreads quickly. It can help you make friends and meet new people. I challenge you to do something compassionate today.

One small act of kindness can change the world, and it starts with you. You can make a difference!

CHAPTER 10

Patience

Waiting for Your Chance

Like most people, I'd rather not wait for anything. But over the years, I have learned that patience is such an important quality, and it takes time to achieve anything that truly matters in your life. For example, learning to play the guitar wasn't easy. It took me a long time to learn how to play certain chords and patterns. But because I kept working at it, I can now play almost anything!

Patience is having the ability to accept and keep working through challenges or frustrating situations without getting angry or upset. I would never be the guitarist or songwriter I am today had I gotten annoyed every time I couldn't perfectly play a chord (because the truth is, that happened a lot). But I stuck with it, and it paid off. When you are patient, you show self-control and recognize that putting the time and effort into your goals or hobbies is actually just part of the journey.

Success doesn't happen at the snap of a finger or overnight. The Wright brothers, who invented the first powered flying aircraft, spent years of planning and testing to create their first prototype. Once NASA decided to put a human on the moon, it took almost six years to achieve the feat!

. . . .

ALL THESE AMAZING ACCOMPLISHMENTS WOULD NEVER HAVE OCCURRED IF SOME OF OUR GREATEST THINKERS AND INVENTORS WEREN'T SUPER PATIENT.

. . . .

I started to play the guitar and write my own songs when I was ten years old, but I've been singing from the time I was very little. I've always wanted to perform. It became my dream to share my music on the biggest stages in the world. I have worked hard to reach that goal. When I really got serious about my music career at age eleven, many people told me that I had to move to Nashville, which is sort of like the home of songwriting and country music. Getting a recording contract there would get me one step closer to letting the world hear my music.

There were a few times over the years when I met with record labels, but because I was so young, they wanted me to wait before signing me to a deal. It was really hard for me, because I was so eager to accomplish my dream, but instead of getting discouraged, I just kept practicing and practicing. Eventually, at age sixteen, I was lucky enough to get an interview with Creative Artists Agency, a famous talent agency. It has offices in New York, Los Angeles, London, and of course Nashville.

My mom and I flew to Nashville in the middle of fall and met with one of the top country music and rock agents in the world. I was nervous, but it went really well. I didn't expect a whole lot, and I was used to the disappointment of being told to wait until I'm more developed as a writer or singer or guitarist (aka when I'm older). So I went to the first meeting and performed some of my songs for the agent, and he said, "You know what—I would like to meet with you again." Although I was excited about this, I still had feelings of doubt because I wasn't sure what he was thinking.

It wasn't long before my mom and I flew back to Nashville for another meeting. This time I talked about Savannah's Soldiers, the thousands of kids our organization had inspired, and this very book. I couldn't believe it when the agent said, "I thought you were a kid with just a dream to sing. I didn't realize that you had worked so hard on all of these projects. I'm confident enough to tell you to move

to Nashville. I want to sign you and work with you directly. You are going to be a part of CAA."

This was the biggest YES I could've received from the biggest person in Nashville! I tried not to cry as we took pictures with him in front of the Creative Artists Agency sign in his penthouse office above the city that I had already fallen in love with.

The rest is history. I am writing this book while moving with my mom from Florida to Nashville. I haven't gotten a record deal yet, but I know it will happen one day. It took me most of my life just to get to this point. But my patience, even through the tough times, proved to everyone around me that I would eventually get from "here" to "there." All of the blood, sweat, and tears were worth it.

Over the years I've learned a lot about different ways that you can stay determined to keep working for your dreams, even when you really just want to get there.

ONE OF MY FAVORITE WAYS TO KEEP FOCUSED IS TO CREATE A "DREAM BIG" BOARD.

A Dream Big board is a place where you can put lots of pictures and images of your dreams and goals.

Dream Big Board

- - - - - - - - - - - - - - - - - - -

YOU'LL NEED A FEW MATERIALS:

— Large craft board, poster board, chalkboard, or corkboard

— Scissors

— Tape or thumbtacks

— Markers or crayons

— Leftover magazines or newspapers (you can even print pictures from the Internet with the help of an adult)

HERE IS MY FAVORITE WAY TO CREATE A DREAM BIG BOARD:

1. Start by drawing a big line down the middle of your craft board, poster board, chalkboard, or corkboard.

2. On the top of the left side, write the word "Dreams." Then, on the top of the right side, write the word "Accomplishments."

3. **Cut out pictures that represent the goals or the dreams you'd like to see come true. Put those pictures on the "Dreams" side of your Dream Big board.**

4. **When you reach a goal, move that picture to the "Accomplishments" side of your board.**

You might want to put pictures of a house, a beach or a snow-covered mountain, a car, the college you want to attend, a famous person you would love to meet, or maybe a singer, a musician, or an actor you really respect. If you love sports, you could put a picture of your favorite athlete or a soccer ball or basketball.

Each of these pictures should represent something that is really important to you . . . that you've made a goal for yourself to achieve. For example, my Dream Big board had pictures of Nashville, country and pop singers, instruments (like a guitar), my best friends (to make me smile when I'm feeling discouraged), places I want to perform (like Madison Square Garden), and even pictures of some of the record labels I would love to sign with.

I tacked them in and left them there. As I worked hard to accomplish these big goals, I moved the pictures closer to the middle.

Then when I finally reached a goal—like learning to play the guitar, for example—I moved that over to my "Accomplishments" side of the board. It is so cool to look at the board each day and track your progress. I also love seeing what I have accomplished with my hard work and patience, and what I am still working hard to obtain.

A Dream Big board keeps you focused and reminds you why you are putting in all the effort and energy. The best part is that you can add dreams to it and take them away as your interests change.

Another cool thing you can do? Take a picture of your Dream Big board and include it in your letter to a service member! Show them what you really love to do, and then ask them about their dreams and goals. You can learn a lot about someone this way.

ANYTHING THAT REALLY MATTERS IN LIFE WILL TAKE PATIENCE. DON'T RUSH, AND DON'T EVER GIVE UP.

It is totally normal to get frustrated and angry sometimes, but those are the exact moments where you just have to take a deep breath and let your patience take control. You've got this.

CHAPTER II

Being Thankful

Appreciating Those Who Make the World a Better Place

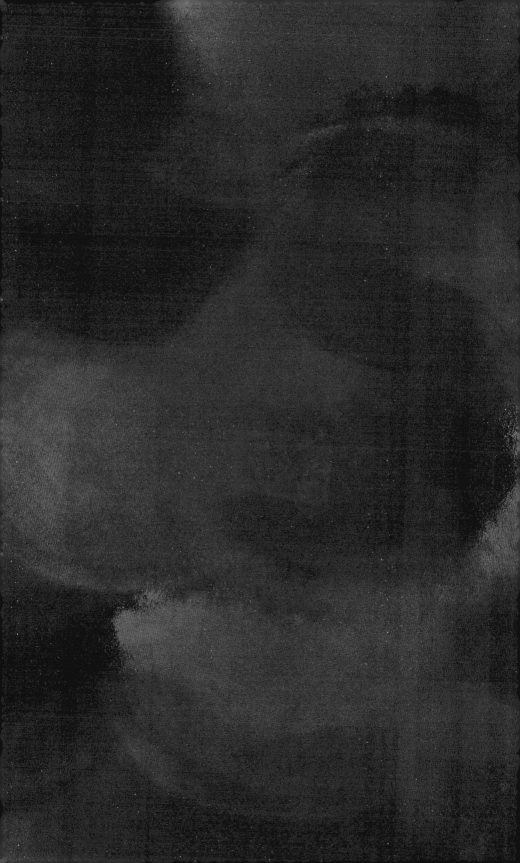

There are a lot of people out there who help to make the world a better place. While Savannah's Soldiers celebrates the tremendous difference our soldiers make, it is important to recognize that we should all feel thankful for the heroes in our local communities as well. Police officers, firefighters, emergency personnel, teachers, nurses, and anyone else who protects us, keeps us safe, and helps us through difficult times. Those are the people, along with our soldiers, we should celebrate every day.

I always get a little nervous when I see a military member, even though I see them often. A lot of times you can pick them out because they are wearing camouflage fatigues and have their last names on their uniforms. I see soldiers at the airport, at the grocery store, at restaurants, even at local coffee shops. The reason I get a little nervous is that even though I don't know them, I always make it a regular practice to walk up to them and thank them for their service. It can be a little intimidating, but it is so important to show service members that we are thankful. I've also paid for their coffee or lunch or bought them a snack at the airport while they waited to board a plane. I've even seen other people buy a tableful of soldiers their meals or offer a soldier their first-class seat at the front of the airplane.

THESE SIMPLE ACTS OF KINDNESS REALLY INSPIRE ME AND MAKE ME SO HAPPY THAT OTHER PEOPLE RECOGNIZE THE SACRIFICES OUR TROOPS MAKE FOR US.

It isn't always easy walking up to someone you don't know, but overcoming your fears can show them how much you care.

The next time you see a military member in the airport or while you're out, consider walking up to them and saying, "Thank you for your service" or "We appreciate you." You can follow either of these phrases with a handshake. It might be intimidating to walk up and say "thank you," but it makes a huge difference!

The same is true for our local heroes like police, fire, and emergency personnel. Restaurants or coffee shops might offer them a meal or a drink on the house, while other people might offer to bring lunch to a fire station. I've seen kids bake brownies for police officers and write nice cards thanking them for all they do for us. The point is that these people risk their lives and take on a lot of responsibility to keep us safe at home and at our schools.

Even as kids, we have so much to be thankful for, and I am not just talking about our troops or our local heroes. Many of us have friends and family who love us so much, and we should be thankful for all they do for us. Studies show that expressing gratitude to the people around you has been linked to overall happiness, stronger relationships, higher self-esteem, and a better outlook on life in general! Increased gratitude helps people feel a greater sense of well-being and reduces feelings of disconnection toward others. If you feel like a friend might be acting distant or disconnected, cheer them up by sending a message of appreciation! It might bring the connection right back.

One of the people I am most thankful for is my mom. She is so amazing and supportive—I could write an entire chapter about all the things she's done for me. I love leaving small notes around the house for her to find that will make her smile. I do the same thing for my sister. Letting someone know you appreciate them, even if it's just a message on a sticky note, can make their entire day.

An Attitude of Gratitude

It's important and powerful to show friends and family that you appreciate them. There are countless ways to do this. You can share art, small notes, and of course letters. Almost every one of my friends spends a lot of time on social media. Snapchat, Instagram, Twitter—there are so many outlets at our fingertips that we can use to show the people around us how much we appreciate them.

One of my favorite methods is to start a gratitude challenge. Thankful Thursdays is one that I really enjoy. Over the course of a month, wake up on each Thursday morning and post three things you are thankful for on your favorite social media outlet. After you post each one, tag it with the phrase #ThankfulThursday. Then challenge three friends to do the same, using the tag #GratitudeChallenge. You are not only showing appreciation to those you care about but also helping your connections do the same.

Thank you!

¡Gracias!

Thanks!

ankfulThursday

what you do!

#GratitudeChallenge

– THANK YOU!!! –

SHOWING SOMEONE THAT YOU ARE THANKFUL FOR THEM IS SUCH A POWERFUL WAY TO BUILD A BRIDGE.

Take some time today to spread gratitude and reflect on people and things that you are thankful for. Send someone a text letting them know you appreciate them, or leave a thank-you note stuck to the fridge for a family member. Bring your teacher a small gift, or write a letter to a sibling to say they're awesome. It's easy to inspire and spread gratitude, so get out there and be thankful!

Thankfulness is the tune of angels.

— Edmund Spenser

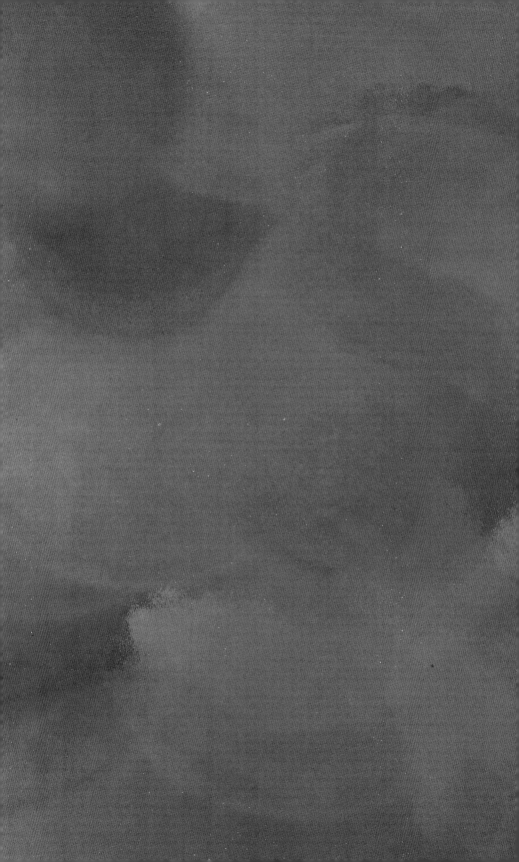

CHAPTER 12

Love

Connection Overcomes Distance

Je t'aime.

Te amo.

Eu te amo.

Ich liebe dich.

As you can see from these different translations of the phrase "I love you," it is truly a universal language. We know that there is a word for love in every language, culture, and country in the world. But when you think about it, what does love really mean? Is it an act of kindness from a stranger? A hug from a close friend? A first kiss?

The truth is that there is not one answer to this question. But what we do know is that love is beautiful because it means something different to every person. We each have our own way to show love and experience it.

I *love* to talk about love. In chapter 9, we discussed compassion, which is really a way to show people around you love by caring about them and helping them through difficult times.

Love is something you can see, you can feel, and you can hear. If compassion is caring for others and hoping things are easy for them, then love is wishing that people are truly happy. If you keep your eyes open, you can see love in everyday moments all around you. Love exists in the tiny moments in our lives. Love is when my neighbor walks his old dog and stops to pet him whenever the dog sits down on the sidewalk because he is tired. It is watching a woman at the park laughing with her little baby and playing peekaboo. It is the smell of a rose from your valentine. It is a home-cooked meal your mom or dad makes for you after a long day at school. The world seems like a much more beautiful place when you notice these small moments of love being shared.

Love is everywhere, and there are tons of opportunities to spread love to the people you care about and to those you might not know yet. As hard as it might be to describe the word "love," it is super easy to show it. You probably show people you love them every single day without even thinking about it.

Wilson was one of the first people who taught me the true definition of love. Her love for her dad inspired me a lot. She was always thinking about what she could do to make sure he was smiling. She would talk about him all the time, and stay up late with her cell phone ringer on just so she could talk to her dad if he called for a few minutes. Since he was on the other side of the world, they were on different schedules. Wilson enjoyed filling him in on what was going on in her life. She also could tell how much he loved hearing her voice and listening to her talk about little everyday things, like what she had for lunch, what she was doing after school, and even who she had a crush on. It was easy for Wilson to show her dad how much she cared for him, even though they were far away from each other. It was a connection that transcended the distance.

I don't think I could write a chapter about love without talking a little bit about my mom and her love for me. My mom always shows me her love, and her complete and nonstop support for my dream to be a singer-songwriter reminds me just how much she cares.

Since I was a little kid just starting to sing and perform, my mom was always by my side. She used to drive me almost two hours each way for my rehearsals and to sing the national anthem at various professional sporting events. She'd sacrifice time with her friends and maybe even going to the gym and doing some of her favorite things so I could practice and get ready for my big performances.

I had more responsibilities as I got older. Mom would fly with me to Nashville to meet with agents, record labels, and vocal coaches so I could further my dream of being a singer. My mom left all of her friends and her hometown in Florida to move us to

Nashville to help me start a career as a professional singer. Her love for me allowed my goals to soar.

Hearts for Our Heroes

Savannah's Soldiers has a special writing initiative called Hearts for our Heroes. Every year around Valentine's Day, we encourage writers to show some extra love toward the military. The troops probably miss their loved ones a little more than usual during this time of year, being so far away from the people they love most.

If you'd like to write to a service member on Valentine's Day, feel free to send your letter or card to me, and I'll get it to a hero who needs love and support from home. But don't stop there—why not share the love with everyone? We've talked a lot about sending messages to people who are far away, but what about the people close to you who you see every day? They deserve a love note too. Here are some tools to show a little bit of extra love toward a hero of yours, near or far.

I have listed some fill-in-the-blank prompts you can use to get started on your own letter to spread the love and show appreciation for anyone you think deserves some.

Dear _____,
(Name of person you admire)

You are so _____ and _____.
(kind, considerate, amazing, thoughtful)

Thank you for _____.
(caring for me, helping me with homework, being a great friend)

I remember the time when _____
_____
(personal experience you had with that person)

I want to tell you how much you mean to me. You are always there to
_____.
(give help when I need it, support me along the way)

You are a great example of _____
_____.
(kindness, courage, love, heroism)

Thank you for everything!

_____,
(With love, With admiration, Your friend, Sincerely)

_____
(Your signature)

Have fun writing your letter and spreading the love to the people around you who mean the most. But you're not done just yet. Next, you get to decorate it and put it in an envelope. Finally, I always try to add to the surprise for the recipient by leaving a letter somewhere I know they'll find it!

HERE ARE SOME OF MY FAVORITE SPOTS:

— On their desk
— Taped to the fridge
— Taped to their bathroom mirror
— Next to where they keep their car keys
— In their backpack
— In their lunch bag
— Between the pages of a book they're currently reading
— Somewhere in their car
— In a gym bag, briefcase, or purse
— On their computer screen or laptop

This is just a small list to get you started. I bet you can think of a lot more places to leave your letter so that your local hero will find it and feel surprised. Keep a running list in your journal and mix it up every time you write a letter.

Valentine's Day is a great day to celebrate love, but you don't have to wait until February. Love is a year-round feeling, so take any opportunity you can to spread it to people who could really use it.

The greatest thing you'll ever learn is just to love and be loved in return.

— Eden Ahbez

CHAPTER 13

Service

Be the Change

When I started Savannah's Soldiers, all I wanted to do was send one service member something to brighten their day and to remind them that people care and are thinking about all our service members.

I didn't set out to change the world or anything; I just wanted to do my part. It wasn't a big deal at the time. But as the days turned into months and my letter-writing campaign started to grow, I found that I deeply loved it. I loved writing letters, recruiting my friends, spreading the word, inspiring others, and setting bigger goals.

I want you to know that, above all, you're never too young to make a difference. As the young members of today's society, we have an exciting opportunity to change the world. We have the ability to connect, to build bridges, and to uplift those around us and help make them happier. It is almost like our responsibility in a lot of ways. If we aren't going to do it, then who will?

YOU'RE *too*

TO MAKE *a*

don't LISTEN TO

LISTEN TO

people who

YOU

the

NEVER

Young

DIFFERENCE;

tell you that

CAN'T CHANGE

World.

There were a lot of times when people told me I was too young to make a difference. They said that one letter wasn't going to do anything. But I knew in my heart that even one small letter would make a difference to the person who opened it, and that is what mattered to me. I wasn't going to get discouraged by other kids or even adults telling me I couldn't make an impression on the world around me. I was already too busy building the bridge. Don't listen to people who tell you that you can't change the world, because my friends and I are proof that you can.

Think about how amazing the world would be if we all decided to make a positive change. This book is meant to help you make a difference, connect to the world around you, and leave the world better than we found it. Just remember what we discovered together—and always be . . .

Sincerely, YOU

1. Find your inspiration.

Feeling inspiration and passion is so important. Pick something you really enjoy and get excited about. When you are passionate about something, you will always do a better job at it.

2. Be resilient.

You have to believe in yourself and never give up. This is an important one. Remember there will always be people who tell you that you can't do it. Don't listen!

3. Build your team.

No one can do it alone. Not any one of us. We all need friends, family, and our community to help make a difference. I started Savannah's Soldiers with the help of my mom and some close friends. Then it spread to our classes, our schools, and eventually all over the country AND internationally. But I never could have done it without such an amazing team.

4. Be courageous.

Heroes face their fears. It might feel scary to get out of your comfort zone to volunteer or start to build something new in your community. But you have to remember you are doing a great service to the world and building meaningful connections in the process. Don't let a big dream or opportunity to help the world around you go unrealized because you are afraid to do something about it.

5. Be prepared.

It really does help to set very detailed and specific goals so you know you are moving in the right direction, and then start practicing. Once you meet your goals, you can change them and make them even greater. It always feels amazing to celebrate reaching your goals.

6. Get creative.

Remember, nothing will happen if you just sit around and talk about it. You have to turn your thoughts into reality. You definitely need to create a good game plan before you hit the ground running, but then you have to take some action. It doesn't have to be huge; start with small steps.

7. Confidence is key.

Being confident is one of the best ways to overcome your fears and reach your goals. It unlocks doors and helps you to find amazing opportunities that might otherwise not happen. When you are confident, you tell the world around you that you are totally present and ready for any challenge that might come your way.

8. Be flexible.

You never know when life is going to throw you a curveball. You often have to adapt to a new situation, so always make sure you have a plan B. Flexibility gives you a number of shots at happiness and allows you to keep moving forward even when things don't go exactly as you planned.

9. Be compassionate.

Compassion is extremely important to us all. We discussed just how important it is to show love to the people you care about the most. It is just as amazing to care for others you might not know as well.

10. Always be patient.

No matter who you are or what you are trying to accomplish, patience is a skill that will help you to get closer to your goals. True patience allows you to wait for a great opportunity and reach your goals undeterred by the hard work, effort, and time they take to achieve.

11. Have an attitude of gratitude.

There are so many things in the world for which we can all be thankful. I am thankful for the support of my entire family and for the opportunity to pursue my dreams as a singer here in Nashville. I am so thankful for the service of the troops protecting our freedoms. What are you thankful for?

12. Show the love.

Love makes the world go around. We connect in many ways with one another, and spreading love through every inch of this world makes a tremendous difference in our happiness and the health of humanity.

It isn't nearly as hard as you might think to make a difference. For me, it all started with something as simple as writing a single letter. Just one piece of construction paper, a few markers, an envelope, and a bunch of stamps. That was it!

It is okay to feel overwhelmed and unsure of where to start. One easy way to get started is to participate in a service project. You'll feel amazing as you help people and connect to the world around you.

Everybody can
be great
because everybody
can serve.

—Martin Luther
King Jr.

SOME OF MY FAVORITE SERVICE PROJECTS

♡ Join Habitat for Humanity and help your local community build a home for a family in need.

♡ Collect lightly used clothes from your neighbors and donate them to people in need.

♡ Set up a weekly or monthly musical performance or play at a senior citizen community.

♡ Organize a food drive in your town or school.

♡ Plan a bake sale or lemonade stand, and donate all the proceeds to a charity you really like.

♡ Dress up like a comic book hero and visit kids at a local children's hospital. Recruit your friends too!

♡ Collect gently used toys from kids at your school and then take them to a family shelter.

♡ Start a weekly breakfast for a veterans hospital. Meet with the veterans there and take notes about their service. Create a collage or short story for each one and send it to them.

♡ Place recycling bins in your school to help kids learn how to protect our planet.

♡ If you live by the shore, organize a monthly beach cleanup (shout-out to Florida!). You and your friends can pick up the trash and debris you see in the sand.

♡ Start a campaign to carpool to school to help reduce harmful emissions going into the environment.

If you have trouble tackling any of these projects, enlist the help of adult family members or your teachers. No doubt they would love to pitch in to help you make a difference.

. . . .

NO MATTER WHAT, DON'T EVER LET ANYONE TELL YOU THAT YOU AREN'T ABLE TO HELP THE WORLD AROUND YOU.

. . . .

Wow! What a journey. Everything in this book is meant to help you to connect, to love, to get more involved, to find greater happiness in helping others, and to change the world. If we all do our part, then the rest will be easy. This is our world, and we all carry a great responsibility to make sure it's a beautiful and happy place for everyone. Let's move mountains.

Be strong and be confident in yourself. I have faith in you.

With love,

SM ♥